HOLIDAY FUN

THANKSGIVING

KIM THOMPSON

NorwoodHouse Press

Cataloging-in-Publication Data

Names: Thompson, Kim.
Title: Thanksgiving / Kim Thompson.
Description: Buffalo, NY : Norwood House Press, 2027. | Series: Holiday fun | Includes glossary and index.
Identifiers: ISBN 9781978580749 (pbk.) | ISBN 9781978580756 (library bound) | ISBN 9781978580763 (ebook)
Subjects: LCSH: Thanksgiving Day--Juvenile literature.
Classification: LCC GT4975.T548 2027 | DDC 394.2649--dc23

Published in 2027 by
Norwood House Press
2544 Clinton Street
Buffalo, NY 14224

Designer: Rhea Magaro
Editor: Tricia Hoffman

Photo credits: Cover, p. 1 Alexander Raths/Shutterstock.com; p. 4 Nastyaofly/Shutterstock.com; pp. 5, 11 Pixel-Shot/Shutterstock.com; p. 7 Aleksandr Dyskin/Shutterstock.com; p. 8 PeopleImages/Shutterstock.com; p. 9 Bespaliy/Shutterstock.com; pp. 13-15 Library of Congress; p. 16 JeniFoto/Shutterstock.com; p. 17 Stock for you/Shutterstock.com; p. 18 barbsimages/Shutterstock.com; p. 19 Drazen Zigic/Shutterstock.com; p. 21 SeventyFour/Shutterstock.com;

Printed in the United States of America

CPSIA compliance information: Batch #CSNHP27: For further information contact Norwood House Press at 1-800-237-9932.

TABLE OF CONTENTS

THANKSGIVING IS HERE!

There is a chill in the air. Good smells waft from the kitchen. You are ready for a big meal.

On this fall **holiday**, people come together to **feast**. It is Thanksgiving!

A SPECIAL DAY

Americans celebrate Thanksgiving every year. It is on the fourth Thursday in November.

MACY'S
PARADE

Farmers have **harvested** their **crops**.

There is a **bounty** of food.

There is corn. There are pumpkins, apples, potatoes, and more.

People are **grateful** for the harvest. They give thanks. That is why *giving* and *thanks* are in *Thanksgiving*!

People remember an event from history. It was more than 400 years ago.

People called Pilgrims crossed the ocean. They came to land that would become America.

American Indians helped the Pilgrims. They showed how to grow crops.

They all got together for a harvest feast.

HOW TO CELEBRATE

Families make special foods. They make American foods like turkey, pumpkin pie, sweet potatoes, and cranberry sauce.

Some families make foods from their cultures. They might make **mole** or **kimchee**.

People watch parades. They run in "turkey trot" races. They watch football games.

Family and friends gather. They talk, laugh, and pray. They eat!

On Thanksgiving, people give thanks.

Everyone has a full belly, and everyone is happy!

GLOSSARY

bounty (BOUN-tee): a big, generous amount of something

crops (krahps): plants grown as food for people and animals

feast (feest): to eat a large, special meal

grateful (GRATE-fuhl): thankful and appreciative

harvested (HAHR-vis-tid): gathered ripe crops from a field or orchard

holiday (HAH-li-day): a special day; a day when most people do not go to school or work because of a religious or national celebration

kimchee (KIM-chee): pickled cabbage and other vegetables; a traditional food from Korea

mole (MOH-lay): a spicy sauce with chiles and chocolate; a traditional food from Mexico

THINKING QUESTIONS

1. When is Thanksgiving?
2. Who celebrates Thanksgiving?
3. Why are people thankful for the harvest?
4. Who were the Pilgrims?
5. What foods are eaten on Thanksgiving?

INDEX

ABOUT THE AUTHOR

Kim Thompson lives in Columbus, Ohio, with her husband and two funny cats. She has written many books for kids. Her favorite Thanksgiving foods are pumpkin pie and mashed potatoes. Her favorite holiday is the one that is coming up next!